21st
Century
Skills Library

COOL CAREERS

GREEN GENERAL CONTRACTOR

BARBARA A. SOMERVILL

WITHDRAWN

Published in the United States of America by
Cherry Lake Publishing, Ann Arbor, Michigan
www.cherrylakepublishing.com

Content Adviser
Lindsay Moody, Owner, Organic Think

Credits
Photos: Cover and page 1, ©iStockphoto.com/lisafx; page 4, ©Photolibrary;
page 7, ©iStockphoto.com/nsj-images; page 8, ©iStockphoto.com/RonTech2000;
page 10, ©Andresr/Shutterstock, Inc.; page 12, ©Juraj Kovacik/Dreamstime.
com; page 15, ©Stanislav Komogorov/Shutterstock, Inc.; page 16, ©Alexander
Fedorov/Dreamstime.com; page 19, ©iStockphoto.com/travellinglight; page 21,
©iStockphoto.com/acilo; page 22, ©iStockphoto.com/tattywelshie; page 24,
©iStockphoto.com/wbritten

Library of Congress Cataloging-in-Publication Data
Somervill, Barbara A.
  Green general contractor/by Barbara A. Somervill.
    p. cm.—(Cool careers)
  Includes bibliographical references and index.
  ISBN-13: 978-1-60279-987-5 (lib. bdg.)
  ISBN-10: 1-60279-987-3 (lib. bdg.)
  1. Sustainable construction—Vocational guidance—Juvenile literature.
2. Contractors' operations—Vocational guidance—Juvenile literature.
I. Title. II. Series.
  TH880.S66 2011
  690.028'6—dc22   2010029535

Cherry Lake Publishing would like to acknowledge
the work of The Partnership for 21st Century Skills.
Please visit www.21stcenturyskills.org for more information.

Printed in the United States of America
Corporate Graphics Inc.
January 2011
CLSP08

COOL CAREERS

TABLE OF CONTENTS

GREEN GENERAL CONTRACTOR

CHAPTER ONE
IT'S NOT EASY BEING GREENSBURG

O n May 4, 2007, a tornado swept through Greensburg, Kansas, destroying 90 percent of the town's

Greensburg residents used the tornado's damage as an opportunity to improve the town.

buildings. Roofs were torn from homes. Fierce winds ripped trees out of the ground and threw them through walls. Bricks and other rubble dotted the streets. This tornado is one of the strongest on record. It left 1,400 people homeless. Greensburg lay in ruin. The community decided to rebuild in a new way. It would turn Greensburg into a green town.

There are many reasons to be interested in green buildings. According to the United States Green Building Council (USGBC), buildings use 40 percent of the country's energy. They also use 13 percent of the country's water. Green buildings reduce energy consumption and water use. This saves natural resources.

Greensburg's citizens wanted their town to become the greenest in America. They hired a green **architectural** firm to design a master plan. The townspeople wanted to rebuild quickly but knew it was worth taking time to "go green."

Greensburg hired green **contractors** to manage the building process. The town's plans called for LEED gold-certified buildings. LEED, which stands for Leadership in Energy and Environmental Design, is the USGBC's set of standards for building quality green homes and public facilities. LEED-certified buildings use less energy and less water. They are built with sustainable and recycled materials whenever possible.

LIFE & CAREER SKILLS

Green contractors need skills that other contractors might not have. They take classes in green building methods and learn about new green products. The National Green Building Program and the USGBC's LEED Accredited Professional (AP) program both offer certification for green builders. Green contractors need these certifications to prove that they are qualified to build environmentally friendly structures.

Many new Greensburg buildings use **wind turbines** to provide energy. Because Kansas is a windy location, plenty of free energy powers the town.

The people of Greensburg chose a style of home from the 12 model houses built by green contractors. The well-**insulated** homes cost less to heat and to cool. They are made of recycled wood. Lawns are filled with native plants instead of grass. These plants are adapted to the environment and require less water than traditional grass. Green contractors installed Energy Star–rated appliances to help save gas and electricity.

Recycled insulation is made from recycled blue jeans or newspapers.

Greensburg is one of the greenest towns in America, but it is not the only place using green contractors. A city does not need to be completely rebuilt to "go green." Green contractors can remodel homes, businesses, and public buildings to make them greener.

Green schools use less energy than regular schools to heat, cool, and light classrooms.

21ST CENTURY CONTENT

The Energy Star program was set up in the United States in 1992. Energy Star appliances use about 20 to 30 percent less energy than regular appliances. Energy Star ratings are also used in Australia, Japan, Canada, New Zealand, Taiwan, and the European Union. Green general contractors install Energy Star products, including dishwashers, refrigerators, and heating systems.

Throughout the world, interest in green building is growing. Some businesses use wind turbines or gas from landfills to help power factories. Green schools, such as Clearview Elementary in Hanover, Pennsylvania, have saved thousands of dollars a year in energy costs. They also use up to 30 percent less water than non-green schools.

In the state of Washington, green builders have developed a green beach town called Seabrook. Seabrook's homes use shingles from a local lumber company. The shingles are made from recycled wood and cedar trees from the building site.

These green factories, schools, and homes can help improve the planet's health and save resources. Every one of these projects needs a green general contractor to supervise it.

CHAPTER TWO
WHAT A GREEN GENERAL CONTRACTOR DOES

A general contractor organizes building projects. She is responsible for making sure the work is done

Contractors make sure a building matches its blueprints.

correctly. She also manages the workers who do the actual building. A contractor's job begins with the blueprints, or plans for a building. It usually ends when the building is finished, but a contractor may sometimes be called back if something needs to be fixed after the building is completed.

Contractors start a project by getting the architect's blueprints. Blueprints show every part of the job, from walls and windows to plumbing and heating. Everything is measured precisely. Blueprints show details for each floor as well as the outsides of the building.

Contractors do not do all of the **construction** work themselves. They hire trade workers such as landscapers, electricians, and plumbers. Each trade worker gives the contractor an estimate for the cost of the job. For example, a plumber gives the contractor an estimate for the pipes, drains, and other parts of the plumbing system. The estimate includes the cost of the building materials and of the plumber's labor. Once a contractor knows what each job will cost, he can determine a total cost for the building. He then makes a bid on the project. A bid is a contractor's offer to provide labor and materials for a certain price.

General contractors must be well organized and schedule their projects carefully. They also need to work well with people. A building project usually has several different trade workers on the job at the same time. As parts of buildings are finished, contractors call in other trade workers to begin their jobs. For example, the electrician must finish wiring the building before the contractor brings the carpenter in to finish the woodwork. Landscapers don't start working until the building is nearly finished.

Some green buildings even have landscaping on their roofs!

A green building does more than just **conserve** resources. It is also safer for the environment. "Green building is really about quality control," says Brandon Weiss, a green general contractor in South Elgin, Illinois. "It's the best way to build, even if you are not an environmentalist."

Dana Kose, a LEED AP from Denver, Colorado, agrees. She notes the importance of recycling, saving energy, and other aspects of green contracting. "I really think most people are catching on to the need for green contracting," she says.

Becoming a green general contractor requires additional education and experience. High school students can prepare by taking math, science, and computer technology classes. In college, future contractors should study construction science, construction management, architecture, or **civil engineering**.

Each state has its own laws about who can be a contractor. In some states, a contractor must pass a test to earn a **license**. Contractors are tested on their knowledge of the trades and on other subjects, such as insurance and safety. Contractors usually must pay exam and licensing fees.

New college graduates probably won't work as contractors for major building projects. Most new contractors start by working for large construction companies. They make building cost estimates. They manage small jobs or purchase materials for larger jobs. This work experience helps new contractors move on to jobs with more responsibility.

LEARNING & INNOVATION SKILLS

The first Green Contracting Summit was held in October 2010, in Fort Worth, Texas. It was part of Contracting Week 2010. Topics included changes in building codes, advances in heating and air conditioning, and new green public policies. The summit provided a place for leading contractors and green experts to share knowledge and discuss issues that face those working in the construction industry. Gatherings such as this one are a great way for contractors to continue learning.

It takes education and experience to become a good contractor.

CHAPTER THREE
HOW DOES A CONTRACTOR GO GREEN?

Traditional contractors and green contractors differ in many ways. Green contractors have more concern for the

Green contractors work to make as little impact on the environment as possible.

environment and use more green building materials. Most green general contractors are also active in environmentalism and work to educate the public about better ways to build.

Dana Kose became interested in green building when she was invited to bid on a government project. She was asked to provide her LEED experience, but she had none. "I didn't know what LEED was, but I figured it out quickly," says Kose. "From there, I learned of the tremendous impacts that buildings have on our environment. The rest is history, because after learning about these impacts, green building became my passion."

For Brandon Weiss, becoming a green contractor was a natural choice. The son of a builder, he often spent time at his father's job sites as a boy. Later, when Weiss played professional basketball overseas, he saw how people in other countries built energy-efficient homes. "I've always been an environmentalist," says Weiss, "and green building seemed the perfect way to go." "Homeowners get a healthier home, a healthier environment in which to live," he explains. "They also save money on utilities."

Green builders consider the environment of the building site. Green contractors try to avoid damaging natural **habitats**. They try to maintain green spaces such as forestlands, meadows, and prairies. People who live and work in green buildings enjoy better air quality and fewer potentially harmful chemicals.

It is important for green contractors to use green materials. Insulation can be produced from recycled newspaper and wood pulp. Flooring can be made from recycled rubber. The latest light bulbs use less energy. Special toilets, sinks, and water fountains use less water. Spray foam insulation helps keep buildings warm in winter and cool in summer. This helps keep energy costs down. Green building materials should not cause allergies or contain toxins. Researchers are often discovering new green materials. Green contractors must keep up with the latest products.

21ST CENTURY CONTENT

Each city or town has its own building codes. These codes make sure buildings are made properly and safely. Many cities and towns are enacting newer, greener codes. In Telluride, Colorado, new and remodeled homes must be more energy and water efficient than old homes. A green contractor has to know the local building codes for every project she works on. She must buy materials and construct buildings that meet current codes.

Manufacturers keep working to improve their green building materials.

Green general contractors can build a green home for about the same cost as a regular home. Of course, some buildings cost more than others. Some green products, such as wind turbines or solar panels, add to the cost of a building. But sometimes they generate more power than the building's owner can use. The extra power can be sold back to the utility company. This means green power sources can quickly pay for themselves.

Most green contractors earn a good salary. It depends on many things, including the size and type of projects the contractor works on. Some earn more than $100,000. Some earn about half that much. Many contractors also earn bonuses. Green contractors work hard for their money. They sometimes have to put in long hours.

21ST CENTURY CONTENT

Passive solar systems use natural sunlight to heat a building. One way to use the sun's heat is to build a solar greenhouse addition on a home. The greenhouse design works so well that some greenhouses get too hot, even in the middle of winter. One solar greenhouse in Plattsburgh, New York, reached a daytime temperature of more than 100°F (38° C) inside when the temperature outside was 20°F (−7° C).

Solar panels can cut a home's energy costs.

CHAPTER FOUR
A GREEN FUTURE

The future of green building couldn't be brighter. Interest in lowering energy costs and preserving natural

Green buildings can be almost any size or style.

resources is growing. Scientists warn about global warming and greenhouse gases. Green building cannot solve these problems, but it is a positive start.

Both the USGBC and the National Association of Home-builders offer classes and certification for green building methods. Students can take part in seminars, join a workshop, and study online. To become a Certified Green Professional or a LEED AP, a contractor must pass a rigorous test. Despite the demands, thousands of people throughout the United States are becoming certified green contractors.

21ST CENTURY CONTENT

The National Association of Home Builders, the Associated General Contractors of America, and the USGBC have gone high-tech. They all have Web sites that offer information about classes and other green resources. All three organizations offer awards for outstanding examples of green building. They also hold green building conferences, where manufacturers show off eco-friendly products.

The advantages of green building are clear. Going green uses recycled or **reclaimed** products to conserve raw materials. It reduces or recycles waste during the building process. Green buildings use less energy and less water. They make use of renewable energy sources such as solar power or wind power. Finally, green building produces a long-lasting, quality product.

Green contractors sometimes work with homeowners to make their houses greener.

Green building was once an expensive luxury. Green materials, architects, and contractors were hard to find. Today, the market for green building is booming. More people are realizing that going green can save them money in the long run while also helping the planet. Federal, local, and state governments are also planning for a green future.

21ST CENTURY CONTENT

Here are some green materials used to build a green, energy-efficient house:

- Energy Star–rated roofing shingles, with partly recycled content
- Insulation made from recycled paper and wood
- Floors and cabinets made from reclaimed wood
- Thermal windows
- Water-conserving toilets
- Insulated concrete block
- Power connection to a wind farm
- Energy Star appliances
- No-mow lawn of rye and fescue grasses

The U.S. government offers tax breaks to builders of new green homes. Tax breaks are also available to those who remodel to meet green standards. The U.S. government has adopted new green guidelines for building and remodeling public structures. Cities and towns are adding green building codes to reduce the use of energy and water. To meet these new standards, many people will hire green contractors. Today's contractors are learning new skills, using innovative materials, and finding jobs that did not previously exist.

Saving energy is a big part of green construction. Green contractors find ways to use renewable sources of energy instead of fossil fuels. According to the Associated General Contractors of America's "Building a Green Future" plan, "Across the country, contractors are finding new work installing wind turbines drilling for **geothermal**, 'planting' solar farms, and connecting new sources of power to existing [power] grids."

Every building project produces waste. In 2003 alone, construction and demolition projects in the United States produced about 154 million metric tons (170 million tons) of waste. This waste is steadily filling up landfills.

Much of that waste can be reclaimed or recycled. Green contractors have found unique ways to reduce the amount of waste they produce. These efforts begin when they clear a building site. Although green builders leave many trees on building sites, they must cut some to make room for the building. Builders can turn these trees into lumber, shingles, or **mulch**. Builders also need to dig holes for foundations. They can save the soil to spread over the site when it is time to landscape.

21ST CENTURY CONTENT

After Hurricane Katrina damaged much of New Orleans in 2005, citizens wanted to rebuild their city. They did not want something modern. They wanted to restore the historic nature of old New Orleans.

In March 2010, hundreds of people met to bring new life to the city's Lower Ninth Ward. Architects, contractors, and many other workers offered their skills to renew the neighborhood—in a green way. The program is called Historic Green. It uses green methods to preserve the look of historic buildings. Green contractors will bring energy efficiency and a healthy environment to old homes.

Green builders recycle waste lumber and plywood. They also recycle papers, metals, and plastics. They reuse windows, doors, and roofing whenever possible. Green builders even recycle concrete as landscaping blocks.

21ST CENTURY CONTENT

Emerging green professionals are the future of green general contracting. The USGBC Emerging Professionals program is geared toward young college graduates. The program is not limited to general contractors. It also serves architects, lawyers, teachers, and other professionals.

Construction trends change with the national economy. In a slow economy, businesses and homeowners are less likely to construct new buildings. Construction increases when the economy improves. Experts predict that the United States will build about 15 million new buildings between 2010 and 2015. Those new buildings will need to use energy and water efficiently. That means that green general contractors will be hard at work.

SOME WELL-KNOWN GREEN CONSTRUCTION ORGANIZATIONS

The **Canada Green Building Council (CaGBC)** is an organization that promotes green construction in Canada. It develops guidelines for green builders. It also offers classes for builders to learn new green building techniques and earn LEED certificates.

The **National Association of Home Builders (NAHB)** is an organization that represents the U.S. building industry. Its National Green Building Program helps teach builders about green construction. It offers certification and standards for builders. This organization also researches new green products and shares that information with green builders around the country.

The **Solar Energy Industries Association (SEIA)** was started in 1974 to promote the use of solar energy. It helps spread information about the benefits of solar power. One way it does this is by working with the government to pass laws that encourage energy efficiency. This group also researches new solar technology.

The **United States Green Building Council (USGBC)** is a nonprofit group that works to increase green construction in the United States. Its LEED program certifies that buildings are energy and water efficient. It also makes sure that the buildings use recycled materials. Each year, the USGBC sponsors the Greenbuild conference, where green experts share their knowledge and green companies demonstrate new products.

GLOSSARY

architectural (ar-kuh-TEK-chu-ruhl) having to do with designing buildings

civil engineering (SIH-vuhl en-juh-NIHR-eeng) designing and constructing public building projects such as roads

conserve (kon-SURV) to use less

construction (kuhn-STRUHK-shuhn) the business of building permanent structures

general contractors (JEN-uh-ruhl KON-trak-turz) people who organize and supervise building projects

geothermal (JEE-oh-THUR-muhl) heat from the beneath the surface of the Earth

habitats (HA-buh-tatss) the places and conditions in which living things live and grow

insulated (IN-suh-LAYT-id) covered with material to prevent hot (or cool) air from escaping

license (LYE-suhnss) a legal permission to do something

mulch (MULCH) a protective covering put on the ground to help maintain soil temperature, retain moisture, prevent weeds, or prevent erosion

reclaimed (ree-CLAYMD) something obtained from a waste product

wind turbines (WYND TUR-bynz) machines that generate energy from wind

FOR MORE INFORMATION

BOOKS

Brezina, Corona. *Jobs in Sustainable Energy.* New York: Rosen Publishing, 2010.

Byers, Ann. *Jobs as Green Builders and Planners.* New York: Rosen Publishing, 2010.

Farrell, Courtney. *Build It Green.* Vero Beach, FL: Rourke Publishing, 2010.

Sirvaitis, Karen. *Seven Wonders of Green Building Technology.* Minneapolis: Twenty-First Century Books, 2010.

WEB SITES

Climate Kids: "Green" General Contractor
climate.nasa.gov/kids/greenCareers/generalContractor
Check out an interview with a green general contractor on this NASA site.

U.S. Department of Energy: Roofus' Solar and Efficient Home
www1.eere.energy.gov/kids/roofus
Learn how green technology can make a home more efficient.

INDEX

ABOUT THE AUTHOR

Barbara A. Somervill is the author of more than 200 children's nonfiction books. Science and the environment are her favorite subjects, so writing about green building was ideal for her. Green building helps conserve natural resources and gives people healthy places to live. She really enjoyed learning about the future of building construction, and was particularly pleased to learn that green general contractors are building green schools today.